CHILDREN
FACING GRIEF

D0006124

CHILDREN FACING GRIEF

Letters from bereaved brothers and sisters

Janis Loomis Romond

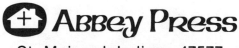 ABBEY PRESS
St. Meinrad, Indiana 47577

Cover Design:
Scott Wannemuehler

Library of Congress Catalog Number
88-83363

ISBN 0-87029-221-8

Published by Abbey Press
St. Meinrad Archabbey
St. Meinrad, Indiana 47577

For John

Contents

Acknowledgments

I am deeply grateful to Fr. Keith McClellan, O.S.B. and the editorial staff of Abbey Press for their ongoing support, genuine interest in these stories and the children they are written for, and careful attention to every detail in bringing this work to fruition. I would also like to thank the following: Madeleine L'Engle for her inspiring belief in this project, for her wise counsel and continuing encouragement, and for teaching me to wait with hope; John Schneider for his depth of understanding and appreciation of the children's stories as instruments of healing, and for his generous support and knowledgeable input; Nancy Berkowitz for her confident and faithful belief in this work and the power of the child's voice, for encouragement throughout the process, and enormous help in editing and critiquing; family and friends for their faith and love and hope, which were essential contributions to the completion of this work.

Most especially I want to acknowledge the generous and courageous spirits of the children who contributed to this book and the parents who supported them. On behalf of myself and every child who will be helped by your stories and every adult who will have a greater understanding of what it's like for children to lose someone they love, deepest thanks and appreciation to: Susan Rae Barnett; Chris and Dan Clark; Kelly, Thaddeus, Angus, and Arian Glenn; Becky Heise; Brett Henderson; Eric Howell; Megan O'Neill; Lori Peterson; Nat and Josiah Raabe; Annette and Brian Robinson; and Martha and Jack Shaw.

Introduction

When my seven-year-old son died, my surviving son, John, was three-and-a-half years old. At the wake, John picked flowers from the pretty border outside the funeral home and brought them inside to his brother. I didn't have the heart to scold him. He placed them in Mark's hands with the Star Wars figures and said good-bye. We had explained to John that "good-bye" is what funerals are about. Mark could never come home again.

At three-and-a-half, John could say the words he was hearing all around him, words like good-bye, dead and alive, never and forever, heaven and earth. But it was hard to tell what these words meant to him. He had questions—painful questions. I know; they were the same ones I was asking myself.

"Why?" John asked. "Why did Mark die? Why couldn't the doctors fix him? Why did God let him die? Where is he? When can he come home? Why can't he come home? How long is forever?" We answered his questions as best we could. We hugged him and ached with him. But we felt helpless trying to explain to him what we couldn't explain to ourselves. Where were the right words?

One night, after months of dealing with these haunting questions, I sat listening to John's bedtime prayer of thanks. "Thank you, God," he murmured, "for Mark when we had him." And then there was a long pause followed by an insistent question: "But why are you keeping him so long?"

John's playmates were asking the same kinds of questions about their friend's big brother, and they often played out their answers. One day when I went to pick up John at a friend's house, she reported that a fight had broken out while the children were playing "being dead." Apparently there was a lot of disagreement about where Mark was and what he now looked like.

"He's under the ground."

"He is not! He's up in heaven."

"Yeah! He looks like an angel. He's got wings."

"He does not! He looks like himself."

"He does not!"

"Does too!"

We laughed about the outburst, yet I felt a little envious at the direct if combative approach the children had taken to dealing with questions which offered no simple answers. I admired my friend's compassion and courage in allowing the children to explore their questions about death, and I was touched by the children's spontaneous and straightforward acknowledgment of the loss they shared. I was struck then—and have been many times since—by the healing power of other children in John's life who have helped him grieve, sort things out, and survive.

For all of us, surviving meant learning to live in a world that was suddenly very different from the one we had known with Mark in it. For John, it meant that one day he was a little brother and the next day he was an only child. It was a world in which his parents were often lost in sadness and didn't feel like playing when he did. It was a world in which he had the whole backseat of the car to himself but no one to squabble with over territory or possessions. The other bed in his room was now empty, night after night.

As I watched John struggling with his thoughts and feelings about losing his brother and learning to live without him, I wondered what I could do to help him survive. One thing which immensely helped my husband and me cope with our grief was to talk with other bereaved parents. It was no small gift to know that we were not alone in our experience, to hear the stories of other grieving parents and to know they had felt exactly as we did and were surviving. I tried to think of a way I could help John experience this same kind of support, to know he was not alone in losing a brother, to know there were other stories that sounded like his. I decided to talk to the people who would best understand what John was going through: other children who had lost a brother or sister.

Through relatives, friends, neighbors, and friends of friends, I found several families who had lost a child and who had surviving siblings. I talked with these families about my hope to collect the stories of children who had lost a brother or sister and to record their reflections about their loss as a support for other children going through the same experience. The families were eager to help, and the children shared their stories generously and courageously. They were hard stories to tell, but were given without hesitation so other children might read them and feel supported by someone who knows just how they feel.

During the interviews, the children talked about what happened to their brother or sister and what the loss had been like for them. They shared what their feelings had been and how their feelings changed over time. I asked them about what and who helped them survive, what hurt, what they miss about their brother or sister, what changes came into their lives as a result of their loss, how long it hurt, and what they would tell other children to expect.

After completing the interviews, I organized the material into a series of letters from the children. This format seemed to communicate most effectively the personal and powerful child-to-child quality of the messages they contained. The letters are the children's words completely.

In this endeavor, I hope to establish a connection among children trying to survive a shared crisis. I believe that these children can speak to and teach one another in ways that are unique. A child experiencing a similar loss will find here acknowledgment and support in coping and surviving.

The more I talked with these children, however, it became powerfully clear that they were teaching me as well. They taught me that children grieve and that their grief has no timetable. They taught me that although there are consistent themes running through their different stories, their individual expressions of grief have as many faces as the children themselves.

The circumstances of losing a sibling varied considerably from family to family. Some lost a brother or sister to illness, others to accidents. The children were different ages: some were older than the sibling they lost, others younger. Some became only children as a result of their loss, others had additional surviving siblings. A few lost a parent to divorce after losing their brother or sister, a situation which I have learned is not uncommon after the death of a child.

Regardless of the circumstances, however, each story began with a sense of shock and disbelief. "It felt like a punch," says Kelly, describing her reaction to the news of her sister's death. "I just sat there. It was such a shock. I didn't cry."

"At first I believed it 'til the night was over," Nat recalls. "But when I woke up in the morning I said, 'It was all a bad dream.' And I cried when I found out it was true."

Even when death was the expected outcome of a lingering illness, it came as a surprise. "I know it had to happen sometime," says Brett about his sister's death from leukemia. "But I wasn't really expecting it."

Initial experiences of shock gradually gave way to feelings of sadness and, for many, anger and fear. These feelings occurred frequently and intensely at first, and then changed from child to child as time went on. "You learn how it feels to be real sad," says Angus.

Nat pointed out that the capacity for that depth of sadness is something that lasts. "Now I can always get sadder about something than I could before."

Part of the children's sadness was related to confronting the same feeling in their parents. "I started feeling sad right away when I saw my mom crying into Jane's little blanket," says Martha. It was helpful for Martha and the other children to share their sadness with their families. "I remember it was real helpful after Jane died to crawl up on Mom's lap and cry with her. We cried for a long time."

Becky found sharing her parents' sadness helpful because they understood. "They lost a person, too," she quietly points out.

In addition to feeling sad, many children react to their sibling's death with anger, much of which is directed toward God. "I felt mad at God for making Ryan sick and making him die," admits Eric. "I didn't want Ryan to go live with God. I wanted him to still be here."

Becky recalls feeling the same way. "I was mad at God. I used to go to bed at night and ask him why. I didn't like him. I cried and just kept asking him why he did it."

The children admit that their anger toward God diminished over time. For Eric, God became an ally instead of the enemy. He found that going to church helped because they talked about God there: "That's who Ryan lives with and that makes me feel a little better." After awhile, Becky felt the answer to her question was that "God took my brother away for a good purpose." Brett used to blame God but now says, "I realize that if God wanted my sister, then I guess it was the way to go because she died at home in her carriage, so at least it was peaceful." Dan was reassured by his mother's explanation that it was Martin's time to die, that the Lord was ready for him. "The Lord didn't just forget to take care of him," Dan realizes.

For others, God had nothing to do with the loss. "I know lots of people get upset and angry with God if someone in their family dies, but I didn't feel that way," says Martha. "I somehow felt like it wasn't his fault. It was just something that happened. But I felt angry at Jane for dying." Lori expressed similar feelings toward her sister who died: "I was a little mad at Reneé, too, because she left me."

Some children felt guilty about their sibling's death and blamed themselves. Annette felt that if she had been out in the barn with her brother helping him with his chores he wouldn't have died. Lori, too, blamed herself for not being "the best sister anyone could be." It took her several years to stop feeling guilty. "Now, when I watch other sisters, I realize that I was just being like a normal sister would be."

Other children become angry at doctors or at feeling left out during their sibling's illness. After his little sister died of leukemia, Brett admits to feeling "kind of like it was the doctor's fault, that they lied to us because they said she would live to be five and then she died just after that."

Susan Rae spent long hours in the hospital when her brother was sick. "I felt angry when I was waiting in the hall to see Donald. I had to run around the hospital all the time by myself. Like when I had to eat, I had to go down and get it myself. Sometimes I got mad at Donald; sometimes I got mad at my parents. I couldn't communicate with anybody. Really, it was because I felt a little neglected when he was in the hospital. It was lonely."

After her brother's death, she experienced a more generalized kind of anger. "Right after Donald died I would just get mad. I don't know really how. I don't know what I was mad at, but I'd just get mad and I'd throw my dolls and stuff on the floor. The feeling of madness still comes back sometimes, but I don't throw my dolls now."

Another commonly reported feeling is fear. "I felt afraid," remembers Brian. "It's like when you're the only one in your bedroom and you're only about four and you're scared that a monster is going to come out and get you. Something like that."

Brian's fear, like Susan Rae's anger, was generalized.

One specific fear experienced by most children concerns their own death, the death of parents, and the death of other family members. "I was afraid I was going to die or somebody would come and kill me or something like that," says Annette. "It lasted quite awhile and then finally went away. But while it was happening I couldn't sleep and kept crying and everything else."

Martha still worries about her parents when they're a little late coming home and is frequently afraid that something is going to happen to her little brother. "I still get paranoid," she says, "but it's not as scary as right after Jane died."

Bad dreams and nightmares are a problem for many. For some they started soon after their sibling's death; for others, they began a little later. "After Bethany died, I had nightmares," says Thaddeus. "Not right after she died but about six months later. I'd be yelling; I didn't have any control. I thought I was going to go crazy. I was really scared. But now I don't have them anymore."

One fear—a fear that intensified with time—is unique to those children who have lost an older brother or sister. These children are afraid of approaching and being the age at which their sibling died. Ten-year-old Susan Rae explains, "I thought since Donald was twelve when he died I was going to do the same. I think this fear is a little stronger now than it used to be because I'm growing older to that age."

A related fear concerns siblings born after the death of a brother or sister. "When my mom told me that I was going to have another brother or sister after Wende died, I was sort of glad but I sort of didn't want to have another one because I didn't want to lose another one," Brett recalls. After his sister's death, Brett had a little brother and then a little sister. "It was hard to watch them go through the age when Wende got sick and died."

What the children seem to miss most about their siblings who die is having that person to play with, even fight with. "The hardest thing about losing Jane is that I can't play with her," says Jack. Brian misses his brother Jerry because "we did a lot of stuff together. We got in trouble for bouncing on the bed. He showed me how to build things, too. And sometimes we'd fight."

Nat and Josiah miss having the chance to ever meet or hold their little sister, Emily, who was stillborn.

Some children miss having someone to share their bedroom with them; others miss the "bigness" of their family size. Everyone misses "what might have been." Kelly reflects, "If Bethany had lived, my life might be totally different."

I also learned from these children a great deal about what helped them grieve. Sometimes, the same things that hurt also helped: sharing sad feelings with family members, talking about the brother or sister that died, crying, going to the cemetery. Megan speaks for many when she points out, "The hardest part of going through this is the times when you feel alone with your sadness." Talking with her mom helps. "Most of the people I talk to haven't lost a brother or sister. They don't know what the feelings feel like. Eric wasn't my mom's brother—he was her son—but she understands how the sadness feels."

Nat says that letting himself cry was helpful "because if you let yourself cry you feel much better in the end."

Some children find going to the cemetery helps, although it may be difficult at first. "The first time we went to the cemetery was gruesome," recalls Lori. "I don't like cemeteries. But the last time we went I felt more secure. I kind of felt happy, and I talked to Reneé."

Returning to school after a sibling's death is also difficult for many children; they feel awkward about being around classmates, and many are not ready to concentrate again on schoolwork. Once there, however, the children find support. Annette had trouble going to school for a while after Jerry died, but found her friends helped her through that time. "My friends helped me through that and helped me with homework if I needed help. The teacher helped me get through it, too. She was close to Jerry and she just knew what it felt like." Annette also found it helpful that her friends let her choose those times when she felt most comfortable talking about Jerry.

Kelly recalls that it was embarrassing going back to school after her sister died. "Everybody just sat there like, 'What do we say to her?' It's like no one knew how to act now that my sister died. But something that really touched me, that helped me, was when everybody on my bus chipped in a little money and got me this thing of plants." When Dan returned to school, he especially appreciated the handmade cards his classmates gave him saying how sorry they were about his brother's death. Susan Rae appreciated the opportunity to play with other children at school even though their reaction to her brother's death was hurtful. "I think it was better for me when I went back to school after Donald died because there were children there I could play with—like my best friend. But at school they think just because he's dead he's not my brother anymore."

Many children commented on how helpful play was, especially being included in other children's games. "After Ryan died," shares Eric, "I was a little happier if I was around my friends because I had someone to play with. I just needed them to play with me."

Being treated normally is also important. "I didn't need pity from my friends," says Lori. "I wanted them to treat me normally, just like they always had before."

These children found many other activities helpful as well: being included in the services for their lost sibling, writing down their feelings, talking to the sibling who had died, looking at pictures of them, and playing music. Some children were helped by peaceful and happy dreams about the brother or sister they had lost. Becky remembers a dream about her brother Denny. In the dream, Denny was older. "He was okay. When I woke up it was like he was there again—like he was with me."

Besides family, friends, teachers, and classmates, the children mentioned that counselors and members of the clergy were also helpful by their understanding presence, by letting the child talk, and by being accepting of the child's feelings.

Good memories provide one of the strongest helps of all. Memories make it possible for children to keep their siblings in their thoughts and feelings. Two children I spoke with had witnessed the births of the little sisters they lost. Most memories, however, were about more ordinary moments: gifts given, games played, words spoken, even tactile expressions. "I can just feel her," says eleven-year-old Thaddeus of his three-year-old sister. "I can still feel on my chest how it felt to hold her."

Jack's sister died when she was four weeks old. When she would cry, her little hands reminded him of windshield wipers, so he called them "windwipers." After she died, Jack decided to keep a little race car he had bought for her when she was born. "It's plastic and it squeaks."

Arian remembers how her little sister loved butterflies and making dandelion wreaths. "Now, when I see butterflies and dandelions I think of Bethany."

Over time, many children began to realize that they were, in fact, surviving their grief. Decreases in nightmares, increases in ability to concentrate at school, and a softening in the intensity of painful feelings were noticed. "Now I can even think about him sometimes without crying," said Annette.

This does not mean, however, that at some point the children are finally "over it." Many felt that "something inside" has changed forever because of their loss and that it will hurt in some way for the rest of their lives. "It stops hurting when you fall asleep," said Arian.

"One question I have since my sister died," ventures Martha, "is when does it stop hurting? My mom says, 'someday,' and that helps. After five years it still hurts, but not as much as it did. I think it never completely stops hurting, but it doesn't hurt as much."

In the experience of losing a brother or sister, many children find changes in themselves that have to do with their outlook on life. "Reneé's death definitely changed me," says Lori. "I've learned that you have to live your life as best you can because you never know when it's going to end. And I look out for myself more. I'm tougher. I've just gotten to be a stronger person inside and out."

Some find that a new sense of vulnerability resulting from their loss also brings a greater sense of appreciation. Kelly says that when her sister died she began to realize "that little things in life are nice. See them," she tells us. "Don't just ignore them or take them for granted. Realize they're there."

Some children have other realizations as they cope with their loss. "One thing I've learned from Martin's death is the importance of letting go," admits Chris, "the need to let go of what has been in the past."

Dan has learned that he has to go on without his brother. "I figured out when Martin died that my life didn't end when his did."

The one consistent expression which these children's letters convey is love. For them, love remains their final connection to the sister or brother they miss. "Emily is always someplace in

me, even when I don't think about losing her. I will always want
her to be there," says Josiah.

And I believe she will be.

Remember the good things

A letter from Lori

Dear Friend,

My name is Lori Peterson. I'm fourteen years old. When I was eight, my seven-year-old sister, Reneé, died suddenly from a severe viral infection. She was born with a condition that made it hard for her body to fight infections.

I remember the day she died. I was just coming home from school. I had a good day and was really excited and the first thing I asked when I got home was, "Where's NeéNeé?" and my mother told me. At first I thought she was lying to me and then I went downstairs and there was a whole bunch of people around and then I knew my mom wasn't lying and I was really upset.

At the wake I didn't want to look at the body so I stayed out in the hallway and my friends and relatives tried to comfort me. It worked a little but I didn't want to talk or anything. Someone said, "Remember the good things about her," and I thought about it and it really did help. But one of my friends said, "It's not so bad," and I just went into hysteria because I said, "Well, how would you know? It's never happened to you," and she couldn't answer it so I was really mad at her for saying something like that.

Reneé was buried in my dress because some embalming fluid had seeped onto the one she had. I feel good about that because she's got something of mine.

When Reneé died I felt mad at God because I thought that maybe he thought that she'd be better with him than with my family because of how I treated her. So I just blamed him for everything. I was a little mad at Reneé, too, because she left me. And I blamed myself—mostly myself. I felt guilty. I wasn't the best sister anyone could be. She got hurt easily; she fell down. So I tried to teach her how not to cry just because you fall down, and if she didn't get it right I'd scream at her. I was just being a typical sister, but it didn't feel right to me after the fact. I don't feel guilty now because I realize, watching other sisters, that I was just being like a normal sister would be—but it took about two years.

For a while after Reneé died I was afraid her ghost would come and haunt me. It was a big fear. I had a dream that I was awakened by a noise and the door opened and there was a coffin and it opened and there she was in my dress and she said, "I hate you and I'm glad I'm dead because I don't have to put up with you anymore." That's when I couldn't sleep in the room we shared anymore. I'd always have bad dreams so I'd go sleep with my parents until we moved, maybe six months later. I got over it as soon as we moved and I was out of that bedroom. After that I had another dream that she came back to me and said she didn't mean it and she was sorry and that she loved me.

My other fear was that maybe I would die, too. Maybe I had the same condition and nobody told me. I found out about the condition a couple years ago. But after a few days I said, "No, that's stupid. They would have told me by now."

At first after Reneé died I felt kind of out of place with my friends. Then some of my good friends would comfort me and say, "We're really sorry it happened," because Reneé was like a sister to them, too, sort of. When I went back to school I felt better. I didn't need pity from my friends. I just wanted them to understand that I was upset because this was a really bad thing in my life, and they shouldn't feel sorry for me because everybody dies. I figured that out. I wanted them to treat me normally, just like they always had before.

I can't say it was depressing to be with my family after Reneé died because we all tried to comfort each other, but it seemed like my parents were more upset than I was. I just couldn't cry, but my parents could.

The first time we visited the cemetery it was gruesome. I don't like cemeteries. But the last time we went I felt more secure. I kind of felt happy and talked to Reneé. I told her I was doing all right on earth and she'd be proud of me, and that I've got lots of friends and where we live now—stuff like that.

The hardest thing still is not having her here to play with. I really miss what it would be like if she was here. I think, "How would it be? Would we still be living where we were then? How would our family be? How would I be?"

Sometimes I write down my feelings about Reneé and then tear them up. Sometimes I play the piano if I get scared, and that helps. Other times I talk to the dog, or go outside and sit, or just lay on my bed with the feelings, and that helps too. I've written special notes to Reneé like, "I miss you. I wish you were here," or feelings like, "Boy, I met this terrific guy and you'd think he was so sweet." I've torn them all up but I like to share myself with her like she was here.

Almost all the memories I have of Reneé are good, about times we played together. When we went on trips we used to dress alike, and people thought we were twins. I think about times at school and her favorite TV show, "Sesame Street." I remember she didn't like zucchini. I've kept some of her favorite books and her ring and her necklace.

At first when Reneé died I missed her so much. I had no one to fight with and nobody to play with. I was all by myself. It was really lonely. Now the feelings aren't as strong. It's still lonely but not as lonely as at first. I'm still sad but not sad enough to think it's my fault. I don't feel guilty anymore. I don't blame anyone, and I'm not mad at her anymore.

Reneé's death has definitely changed me. I've learned that you have to live your life as best as you can because you never know when it's going to end. And I look out for myself more. I'm tougher. If somebody's trying to harass me I stick up for myself. I stick up for my friends, cousins, relatives, brothers, my parents. I've just gotten to be a stronger person inside and out.

Sincerely,

Lori

Lori

We all hugged each other

Letters from Nat and Josiah

Dear Friend,

My name is Nat and I'm almost thirteen. When I was eleven my sister, Emily, died two days before she was born because there was a knot in the cord that gave her air and food and stuff. When my mother and stepfather told me Emily was dead, I hit the bed really hard and cried and cried. We all hugged each other.

At first I believed it, 'til the night was over. But when I woke up in the morning I said, "It was all a bad dream." Then I cried when I found out it was true.

When I went back to school my teacher had told the class not to mention Emily to me. That was okay because I didn't want to talk to them about it. I didn't feel like doing my schoolwork. I thought the kids shouldn't play games and laugh. They should be sad, too.

I felt mad at God for letting it happen. I knew how sad the family would be if someone else died, and sometimes I was scared that I might die, too.

The hardest thing is that there are so many things I know I could do with Emily that I never can now. I wanted to teach Emily how to pet the cats gently and how to kick a ball back and forth. Now I can't. I wonder where she is and what's happening to her right now.

I wrote a poem for her, and we have it in her album. This is it:

Emily, I love you,
I waited for you
and waited for you
and lost you
and cried
and love you.
Your brother, Nat

5

Now I don't think about her as often as I did a year ago. But when I think back I remember when she kicked my hands through my mom's belly, and I feel sad again. Now I can always get sadder about something than I could before. I never used to think I had a care in the world, and now I take things more seriously.

What helped me get through it was letting myself cry, because if you let yourself cry you feel much better in the end.

It takes a while to get over it. You never get over all the pain, but I don't cry about it a lot anymore. You never stop missing them, but it's not like you think about it all the time anymore. When it first happened it was all I could think about.

I loved Emily before she was born, and I still love her even though I never got to meet her. I'll always love her.

You have to go through the whole experience to know what it's like, but you'll feel better in a while. In a while you won't feel like crying so much anymore.

Your friend,

Nat

Dear Friend,

My name is Josiah. I'm almost eight. When I was six my sister, Emily, died before she was born. I think she was doing a somersault and her cord twisted into a knot and she died.

When my mother told me Emily died, we cried. Everybody cried a lot. My grandparents all came that night. Everybody cried and then we had some dinner.

My brother and I went to my grandmother's house for two days while Mama and Allan went to the hospital for the baby to be born. At my grandmother's, she had some fabric to sew Emily a little snowsuit, but then she never wanted to see the fabric again.

When we came home I felt terrible because I loved Emily and wanted to see her alive, and now I can't. I used to hug my mother when Emily was inside her and say, "I love you, Emily," and I felt Emily kick me. Just thinking about it makes me sad. I wrote her a poem. This is what it is:

Emily, we love you
and we miss you.
I wanted to hold you
and now I'm soooooo sad.

I picked a little tiny maple leaf for her. It was very small. We put it in a special book we made for Emily.

I didn't feel like doing things at school. I felt like going home. At my friend's house, sometimes I would go outside and just sit and look. The worst thing was I wanted her to see me and I wanted to hold her. The worst thing is losing her.

We had a church service and lots and lots of people came. I sat in a pew and cried and cried. Another time we sent up some blue balloons to her, and this year we lit a candle for her.

Sometimes when I think about Emily dying, it makes me worry about the new baby that my mother is going to have. I hope the new baby will be born alive.

It's really terrible at first to lose a baby sister, but you get over it in about a year. What helped me was a letter from another kid who lost a baby sister. It helped me to know how it feels. It felt better to know I wasn't the only one.

Emily is always someplace in me, even when I don't think about losing her. I will never stop loving her. I will always want her to be there.

Your friend,

Josiah

Josiah

I used to sleep in the top bunk

A letter from Eric

Dear Friend,

My name is Eric. I'm six years old. Last summer my brother, Ryan, died from a kind of cancer called lymphoma. He was four years old. He died at the hospital.

He was in the hospital a lot before he died. I visited him and it made me feel real happy to see him. I could play with him. I'd go to the closet with games in it and get something Ryan told me to get. They had a Star Wars game and a Garfield game. One time I wrote him a letter at school when I finished all my work. My grandma came and picked me up and we went to the hospital and I gave it to Ryan. In the letter I said, *"It makes me mad when you're sick because I can't play with you. I can play with you but I can't play lots of things because you can't do lots of things."*

When my mom and dad told me Ryan died I felt sad. And I felt mad at God for making Ryan sick and making him die. I didn't want Ryan to go live with God. I wanted him to still be here. When I saw Ryan the morning he died I felt scared, scared of his body and scared of what he looked like.

I remember we went to church for Ryan's funeral. I think they sung a song and then we went to the graveyard and then people talked to me and then we went home.

We go back to the cemetery sometimes and it feels a little better than when he died. We bring bread to feed the ducks. My mom and dad look at the gravestone and then I look at it for a minute and usually the wreath we put by it always falls down and then we gotta pick it up and then we go feed the ducks. Sometimes I talk to Ryan. I say, "I hope I'm gonna go up to heaven like you did and then I'm gonna see you."

It's not very fun when you lose your brother. It's a little bit lonely. It's like nobody's with me. What I miss most about Ryan is that I don't get to play with him anymore. He played Star Wars with me. We raced outside. He always won because I let

9

him. And we pretended we were going on adventures. We rode bikes together sometimes. I rode my two-wheeler and he'd ride his motorcycle. We got him a little motorcycle with little peddles that you didn't have to push. There was a little white thing to push to make it go by itself. Now I have his motorcycle and some of his Star Wars people. One time Ryan taught me to spell his name. I still remember.

Once I dreamed that Ryan was still alive, and we went on a big adventure. There was a big dragon, and we said if we kill the dragon we can win all the money. So we went down the road and into a hall and we saw a big red light. We saw the dragon, too, and he was asleep and then he woke up and we had bows and arrows and we shot at him and we missed, and he blew fire at us but we had a shield. Then we shot our last bow and arrow at him and we killed him and we got all the money. When I dream about Ryan I feel happy because I think my dream is real and he's back with me.

I used to sleep on the top bunk but I changed my bed to the bottom. When I woke up I'd look over the side and he wouldn't be there. Now I'm on the bottom. I don't have to look.

After Ryan died I was a little happier if I was around my friends because I had someone to play with. I just needed them to play with me. But I don't talk to my friends about Ryan because sometimes they don't even think of him. Sometimes I talk with Mom about Ryan. It makes me feel good because I get to talk to somebody and it makes me feel like Ryan's here. We look at pictures, too, because we have picture albums when he was just a baby. Going to church helps a little bit because they talk about Jesus and God and that's who Ryan lives with and that makes me feel a little better. My grandma said that we would go up to heaven sometime and see him again and that makes me feel a little better, too.

I liked Ryan. And he liked me. Ryan was a good kid. At first when he died it hurt a lot. Now it hurts a little bit.

Love,

Eric

Eric

Let go of what has been

Dear Friend,

My name is Chris. I'm fifteen years old. When I was eleven my brother, Martin, died. He was nine years old. He died from a seizure he had during the night at a hospital for mentally handicapped kids where he lived. The hospital was about an hour away from our house. Here's a picture taken a month before he died—Martin's in the front with my sister, Vicky, and I'm behind her with my brother, Dan, and other sister, Tryn. Martin had severe epilepsy and was brain damaged ever since he was a year-and-a-half old, when he started to have seizures. Throughout his life his mind was kind of blocked at a year-and-a-half so he couldn't talk very well and he could barely learn anything. We knew his life was in jeopardy always, but still, when he died, it just kind of took us by surprise.

When I found out Martin had died I was kind of sad, but I wasn't really distraught because he lived away from our home. I think it was easier than it would be for someone who lived in the same house, someone you saw one day and then heard they died the next day and just never saw them again and they were gone.

I think I could accept it better chiefly because I was so young. I have more trouble dealing with it now, I think. As a young kid I felt him kind of a bother because when you tried to tell him something not to do he wouldn't really understand because his mind was kind of in a lock. That was my young-child understanding of him. But as I got a little older and we didn't have him in the house I felt really good when we went to see him. So that was the sadness that I did feel when I heard that he had passed away. There was relief, too, when he died. Now we don't worry about him because he's not there.

When we went to the funeral we saw Martin's body in the coffin before he was buried. I feel good now that I saw his body

11

because I know for fact that he died. It was like, "There's the shell. He's gone."

The funeral service was outside on a bright, sunny day and I remember the hole was already dug and the coffin was above the big hole. I asked to recite the Twenty-third Psalm, but I don't remember much what was said besides that. The next time we went back, the coffin was covered over and we saw flowers. After awhile we came back to see the finished nice neat gravestone. For a long time it was just dirt there and finally the grass grew over it.

Visiting the grave was kind of neat—kind of interesting. We'd look at it, and when we were young kids we'd go around the graveyard looking at other gravestones and trying to find funny names. But it was always kind of nice for us to gather around Martin's gravestone and talk.

After the burial, we had a huge memorial service in our backyard where my mom's uncle came to do the sermon. I remember him saying things about Martin being a child—something about innocence. Near the end he said that there might come a day when we'd go to heaven and we'd see him and he'd say, "I have many things to tell you. Come and let me show you around." It was a good sermon.

My mom's grandmother died about a week before Martin did and I like to think of her first job as being to take care of Martin. I think of where they are as a place. I've always had sort of a picture of heaven; it's a very big place. There's a huge house and a wonderful garden around it, a place where kids can play and adults could relax.

I don't really know about God's role in Martin's death but I'm not angry at God. Because of Martin's condition I think he's better off where he is rather than feeling angry at anyone for taking him.

One thing I've learned from Martin's death is the importance of letting go, the need to let go of what has been in the past. You can't dwell on something like that for the rest of your life because then that's two lives lost, you know. It's just necessary to accept it. I've kind of associated this with my leaving home someday. You know, you can't hang on to them forever. I don't usually think of Martin when I think of leaving home but there is a parallel there. Maybe some kids my age have learned about letting go if they've had an experience similar to mine. Maybe some kids will learn it when they leave home or maybe some people don't ever learn. Martin's death has taught me that nothing lasts forever.

Sincerely,

Christopher

Chris

Dear Friend,

My name is Dan. I am eleven years old. When I was seven, my nine-year-old brother, Martin, died from a seizure he had during the night. He had seizures pretty often, but this time he just stopped breathing and died. It was pretty much a surprise.

When Martin was really little he got sick and that caused him to have seizures and that made him brain-damaged. When I was three or four we would go visit Martin at a respite home near where we lived. Me and my sister would play on the slide. When I was five we moved and Martin went to live at a hospital for brain-damaged people, and that's where he lived until he died. I would have taken it harder if he lived at home because I'd be with him every day.

When Martin died my mom took me and told me the Lord was ready for him and it was his time. Martin didn't just die by accident. The Lord didn't just forget to take care of him and he just died. I think the Lord was ready.

After Martin died we went to the funeral home. They had a nice white coffin and the top half was open and he was just lying there. I didn't feel like crying because the Lord was ready for him.

The funeral was outside. His coffin was on bars over the hole. My great-uncle Frank ministered it. It was just our family, and my brother, Chris, recited "The Lord is our shepherd."

Sometimes we visit the cemetery. It isn't really sad or anything because it's just a shell. Martin's soul is in heaven.

My great-grandmother died somewhere around the same time Martin did and all the kids in my class gave me cards saying

"I'm sorry your great-grandmother and your brother died." They gave them to me in class when I went back. They just kept on treating me normal. In school we do book reports and my friend did one on a book called *My Brother Is Special*. It's about a mentally retarded boy and that reminded me of Martin.

I figured out when Martin died that my life didn't end when his did.

Sincerely,

Dan

Little things you love can't stay forever

Letters from Kelly, Thaddeus,
Angus, and Arian

Dear Friend,

My name is Kelly. I'm fourteen years old. When I was thirteen, my three-year-old sister, Bethany, was killed in an automobile accident.

I'm really proud of this picture of me holding Bethany, surrounded by my brothers Thaddeus and Angus, and my sister Arian. I found out about the accident a couple hours after it happened. I was at a friend's house where I had slept over. My brother called. He was crying. At first I thought it was a joke but he wouldn't cry if it was a joke. I just sat there. It was such a shock. I didn't cry. Then someone came and picked me up and brought me back.

We had two services for Bethany. The first was just for the family early in the morning to bury her. The second was later in the afternoon for everyone. It was at her grave and all sorts of people came. My mom wanted to let balloons go, so some people let hundreds of balloons go at the end of the ceremony. It's something my mom would do. It's probably the first time it's ever been done. It meant something to people. My mom said that people were telling her that now they can't see balloons without starting to cry. It was neat and it was different and it will always stick out in my mind.

Sometimes I wish Bethany was around. When I'm up at the grave or if there's a little kid I see that looks a lot like her, I'll have that feeling of not being able to have a little kid with me. There's an empty hole. I was used to having her around. Sometimes when I'm trying to fall asleep and everything is rushing through my mind, I think about her, how she used to come into my room with her stinky diaper on and crawl into bed with me. I miss her then.

When she first died or even still when I turn the music up

when no one's home, I think I better turn it down because the baby's sleeping. I remember turning it up when I shouldn't, when she was sleeping. Then after she died I thought I shouldn't have done that but now I can.

I was just talking to my friend and she said she saw an attitude change in me after Bethany died, that my attitude got worse and I was more negative. I'm not sure. I just thought about it and I haven't been able to figure it out. I guess that maybe after she died I just didn't care anymore and I talked about it more.

It was embarrassing to go back to school after Bethany died because everybody just sat there like, "What do we say to her?" It's like no one knew how to act now that my sister had died. But something that really touched me, that helped me, was when everybody on my bus chipped in a little money and got me this thing of plants, like seven different kinds of plants. It was just really nice because a lot of these plants are really neat looking and it's just something that found it's way to my heart out of all the other things.

One special memory I have of Bethany is seeing her being born. My mom had her at home. It's something you don't get to see every day—a small miracle kind of thing. The first thing I saw was her head all gray and wrinkly like a worm or something. I just sat there wondering what this person was going to be like in a couple of years. It was neat.

I just realized when she died that little things in life are nice. See them—don't just ignore them or take them for granted. Realize they're there. Get those little pleasures from them.

When Bethany died it was like a punch to me when I first found out and then all of a sudden I was just back having a normal life kind of feeling, and it's been like that ever since. Just always in the back of my head there's this little thing that I remember Bethany, this feeling way down deep inside that I miss her. If she had lived, my life might be totally different.

I've just kind of gone on with life. I don't ignore the fact but it doesn't come up that often for me. You get over the pain eventually.

A bereaved older sister,

Kelly

Kelly

Dear Friend,

My name is Thaddeus. I'm eleven years old. When I was ten, my three-year-old sister died in a car accident.

I came home from my friend's house, and no one was home except for a good friend of our family and her kids. I went in and she said my dad and Bethany were in a car accident. I said, "Oh, I hope they're not hurt." She said, "Yeah, me too." I kept on asking questions and finally she said, "Thaddeus, I have to tell you the truth. Bethany . . . the van rolled over and Bethany and your dad flew out and the van tipped over."

Then I started thinking, "Oh no, I wonder what happened." Then she said that Bethany was unconscious, and I'm looking at her and I said, "She's dead?" and she said, "Yes." She told me how it happened, that Bethany was kind of unconscious for like twenty minutes and then she died in my dad's arms.

The funeral service was up on a hill by our church. It's a really nice graveyard. We just started a church up here so maybe only one other person has died. When the service was over, Mom went up and cut a ribbon with three helium balloons and a wreath on it and they just lifted up and then landed right on my dad's lap, and that was neat. At the end about two hundred helium balloons all went up. It was happy and sad at the same time. We had to let Bethany go—sort of like the balloons.

Bethany's friend, Edmund, had fallen asleep when this all happened. The balloons went off to the east and Edmund lived to the west. He was very sad the next day and he went outside and a green balloon just came right down to him. It's a miracle. We couldn't believe it.

After Bethany died I had nightmares—not right after she died but about six months later. I'd be yelling. I didn't have any control. I thought I was going to go crazy. I was really scared. It happened in dreams but it also happened in the day. All of a sudden I'd be doing something and I didn't know how loud I was talking and I started acting weird. But I don't have them anymore.

It's hard not having her around. I wish she was here to play with. I can still feel on my chest how it felt to hold her. I can just feel her. I can remember the way she walked, kind of thump-thump on the floor. I can hear that.

When your sister dies it's like a big part of your life has been taken away. It's sad. It helped to talk to my mom and dad or cry or take a walk. Ever since my nightmares stopped I'm used to Bethany being dead. When I'm doing something I forget. Even though it's sad, I can be happy for Bethany. She's safe.

At the beginning after she died it was really hard. I couldn't believe it happened. But now I can accept it.

From a friend,

Thaddeus

Thaddeus

Dear Friend,

My name is Angus. I'm nine years old. When I was eight, my three-year-old sister, Bethany, died in an automobile accident. She was coming home from an auction with my dad, and the van hit a wire or something and flipped over and they both fell out. Bethany fell under the van. My dad got her out and held her but when the ambulance came it was too late. She was dead.

My mom and my sister and me were coming home in our other car and on the way home mom said we had to wash the car, and I wasn't too happy about that. So we just went along and we got home and my brother and some other people were all there and I went inside and Thaddeus said there was an accident. So I go, "Oh, no," and he said that Bethany was hurt and she was up with the Lord and I said, "Huh?" and Thaddeus goes, "She's dead." I started crying and I went outside and saw Mom crying with her head in her lap and I asked her if we still had to wash the car and she said no.

At the end of the funeral service at Bethany's grave, our cousin and our friends let about two hundred helium balloons go from up on a hill behind the grave. When the balloons went up my mom let go of a small bunch of balloons attached to a bouquet. It went up and then it went down to where my dad was because it was too heavy. It was like Bethany was leaving the bouquet to my dad. It fell in his lap. Real neat.

Bethany's friend, Edmund, missed the balloons going off because he fell asleep. The balloons went off one way and he lives in the opposite direction. The next morning he woke up and was real sad and he went outside and he saw a green balloon sitting in his yard. He said, "Look what I found in the yard. A balloon came down from heaven from Bethany." It was neat.

I miss Bethany most when I wake up in the morning, having her crawl into my bed like she used to when she woke up. Some days I feel sad and I just cry and cry. It helps to cry. Sometimes I'm angry that she isn't there.

I remember Bethany's chubby cheeks and red hair. She was sort of short and lovable. It helps to see pictures of her. Like this one picture, if you stare at it sometimes she'll just smile at you.

I think Bethany's up with the Lord now. I think she's happy and loved.

It's real hard when your sister dies. You learn how it feels to be real sad. But it doesn't hurt as much now as it did at first. After a while it feels better.

Much love, your friend,

Angus

Angus

Dear Friend,

My name is Arian. I'm seven years old. Last year my little sister, Bethany, died in a car accident. She was three years old.

I remember coming home from an auction we were at and there were lots of people at our house and everybody was crying and I was wondering what was happening and my mom told me. It was so sudden I didn't know what to do.

When we buried her it was Monday, so I missed some school. At the burial everybody just stood around while she was lowered down. Everybody put the dirt over her. After the service at the grave all these colored balloons started coming off the hill and shooting up. They were helium balloons. Bethany's friend, Edmund, fell asleep when the balloons went off and when he woke up the next morning he was crying because he wanted to see the balloons go off. And guess what? He was playing in his yard and a green balloon fell down. He goes, "Look, a balloon. Bethany sent it from heaven." It's true, too.

Bethany's bed used to be in my room. Sometimes I would just look over and wish she was there. In the night time is the time I get to rest and really get to think about it. Sometimes I cry. It's okay to cry. It stops hurting when you fall asleep.

I remember that me and Bethany would always play with flowers a lot. We'd try making wreaths out of them. Sometimes we'd take dandelions and stick them in our shoes, and I remember Bethany loved butterflies. She'd say, "Oh look at the butterfly," if she ever saw one. Now when I see butterflies and dandelions I think of Bethany.

One day after Bethany died I said, "Well she's gone." So she's gone and you just have to live with it. She's not going to come back, and I'll have to go to her if I want to see her.

I think Bethany is in the world of spirits. She's happy and there's angels with her. I think she's older already. You can sort of turn older there.

When Bethany died it taught me that little things you love can't stay forever.

From one of your best friends,

Arian

I know what you're going through

A letter from Susan Rae

Dear Friend,

My name is Susan Rae. I'm ten years old. When I was nine, my twelve-year-old brother, Donald, died from a brain tumor. He was sick for over a year before he died. I didn't know he was going to die. No one told me that they predicted it.

The time that he was sick was so confusing that I'd wish I was sick instead of him. I hated to see my brother in pain. He was in the hospital a lot. That was our second home. I felt angry when I was in the hall waiting 'til I could see him. I had to run around the hospital all the time by myself—like when I had to eat I had to go down and get it myself. Sometimes I got mad at Donald. Sometimes I got mad at my parents. I couldn't communicate with anybody. Really, it was because I felt a little neglected when he was in the hospital. It was lonely.

On the day he died we went to the hospital and they sent me out in the lobby and my parents went in a room near Donald's. The nurses and doctors were in the room with Donald. I couldn't hardly hold in my crying, but I was afraid to cry. Then the minister came and got me and took me in the room where my parents were and I burst out with tears. Momma said she wasn't going to jump to conclusions because she didn't know whether he was dead or not. Then the nurse came out and said they couldn't do nothing with him and he was dead. I had the thought in my mind what it would be like to be alone, and I couldn't believe it.

It seemed like the funeral passed by quick. When he was in his casket I touched him and he was kind of cold. We took pictures. His hair looked like it had been cut a little bit.

When Donald died I would just get mad. I don't know really how. I don't know what I was mad at but I'd throw my dolls and stuff on the floor. The feeling of madness still comes back sometimes, but I don't throw my dolls now.

After Donald died I started feeling afraid of a trail we used to walk on all the time. Now I can't hardly go on it, it's so scary. I guess it's because we went there a lot together, and then he died. And it's scary now to stay up and watch monster movies on the late show on Friday night like we used to. I don't stay up as late as I did with Donald.

The other scary feeling I have since Donald died is about myself dying. I thought since he was twelve when he died that I was going to do the same. It seemed like I almost had to because Momma was making plans for me like she did for him. Like she'd say she wanted him to be a basketball player and she wanted me to be a cheerleader or maybe a teacher and stuff like that. So then I said to myself, "That must be a true sign that I will die, too." I think this fear is a little stronger now than it used to be because I'm growing older to that age.

The hardest thing about Donald dying is that I miss playing with him and watching the late show. I'm used to playing with somebody. When I'm playing by myself, I have to make it two people. I have to pretend I'm with somebody and I have to talk to myself. If I play with somebody, it reminds me of playing with Donald.

I remember that Donald taught me my ABCs. And we used to go wading in the water together. He'd throw rocks at a snake that would sit on a branch right in front of our house and knock it in the water. We'd go fishing for crawl-daddies and sell them for money unless it was a big one.

I think it was better for me when I went back to school after Donald died because there were children there I could play with, like my best friend. But at school they think just because he's dead he's not my brother no more. Like if we're doing family projects, I'll put Donald's name to it and they'll say, "He's not your brother anymore. He's dead." But that doesn't mean he's not my brother. I don't have anyone at school to talk with about Donald. He died in June and when we got back in school they wouldn't say a word about him. It was like a tornado just whipped through their minds and took it away.

I don't have dreams about Donald at night but sometimes I have daydreams. I daydream what it would be like when he gets a little older driving in the car, and I'd be going with him to the store. I wonder what was his future ahead and stuff like that.

Going to the cemetery is really a sad time because there's usually a lot of crying. Sometimes I wish I didn't go, but sometimes I want to go because I want to see the grave and it helps a little bit. I'm just startled when I look at his grave and I say, "This is my brother."

It hurts more now, I guess, because I didn't know much about death at first, but now I'm learning the real facts about it—that you'll never see them again unless you go where they're at. Sometimes when I'm sad, I talk to my parents and it helps a little bit to be sad together. It helps a lot to have other kids to play with. And it helped to read a book called *Children Aren't Like Paper Dolls*. It helped to know other kids felt that way when their brother or sister died.

I wish I had other kids to talk with about Donald dying. I know what you're going through.

Your true friend,

Susan Rae

Susan Rae

A part of your life is missing

A letter from Becky

Dear Friend,

My name is Becky. I'm ten years old. When I was seven, my ten-year-old brother, Denny, suffocated in a corn bin on our farm. My dad and mom came and tried to get him out. Then my aunt called the ambulance. They cut holes in the corn bin and took him out. They tried to save him. They took him to the hospital. I was waiting at my aunt and uncle's house. It was scary waiting to hear. About an hour later my mom came and told me Denny died.

The night he died we all slept in the same bed and every once in awhile, about every hour it seemed like, Mom would get up and go out in the kitchen and do something just to get her mind off it, but she couldn't.

At the wake there were lots of friends and people I know. They were real nice. They were sorry. They said, "He'll be in good hands," and stuff like that. I remember when they carried him down the steps of the church and my dad and my cousin carried the coffin. The minister said stuff like, "Denny was a nice guy and we had lots of fun times and bad times with him"—the usual things.

At the cemetery I kept thinking, "It's not true. It's just a bad dream." They put him down in that big box. Oh, I hated that. I wished it'd never happened. It was like they were shoving him off for a long time and he couldn't get out or something.

I was mad at God. I used to go to bed at night and ask him why. I didn't like him. I cried and just kept asking him why he did it. I don't feel that way anymore because I know he took my brother away for a good purpose.

Going back to school was real lonely, like no one would care or anything, like you didn't have a friend in the world. But two of my real good friends are always willing to listen to me. Sometimes they say I shouldn't think about it. Sometimes they say I should.

I was scared that something would happen to me after Denny died. And I was scared for other people, too. Like when we were out fishing I was scared because my grandpa couldn't swim. I thought if the boat started sinking, what would I do?

One night I woke up in the middle of the night because I had a bad nightmare. It felt like Denny was there again because my nightmare involved him. I was all alone in the bed so it scared me. I was thinking everyone else was gone.

One time I had a dream about Denny coming back. We always used to go fishing out there and this boat came along and he was in it. He seemed older. He was okay. When I woke up it was like he was there again, like he was with me.

It was sad when we had to go up and clean his room. My mom would find stuff and she'd start crying. Like some pictures he drew with markers and stuff that would say, "To Mom. Happy Valentine's Day." She found a lot of things he made that she didn't even know about.

When I was little, Denny taught me how to color, how to stay in the lines. Sometimes he'd hold my hands and show me. He helped me learn to ride a bike, too. When I fell down he'd come over and say, "Oh, you're doing great," and that'd make me feel like, "Oh, boy!"

Sometimes we fought. One time he hit me with a toy box. I got the scar to prove it. Sometimes we had good times and sometimes we had bad times.

I remember there was this real big bully we had in our school and he'd go around pushing everybody around. He pushed me down one day when I had my new clothes on after Christmas, and my brother came up and asked me what happened. My knee had a big hole in it and I said this big guy pushed me down. My brother was looking around and he goes, "Which one?" and he went over and says, "Don't ever touch my sister again," and that guy left me alone.

I miss Denny a lot when I'm sick. He'd always read to me at night if I didn't feel good and he'd cheer me up a lot. He'd tell me what was going on at school and how good I was going to feel when I got better. He'd make me feel like I was real special.

When I feel down about Denny dying I talk to my mom and dad and that helps a lot. I can cry with them because they understand. They lost a person, too.

When your brother dies it's hard to accept. For about a month or so life slows down to a slower pace or something. It's like there's a part of your heart missing and a part of your life is missing, too. It feels like you're the only person in the whole world who's lost anybody, like no one would understand. After three years it's a little easier because I know he was taken away for some good purpose.

Your friend,

Becky

Becky

Things don't seem like they really are for a while

Letters from Martha and
Jack

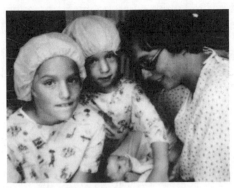

Dear Friend,

My name is Martha. I'm twelve years old. When I was almost eight, my baby sister, Jane, died of Sudden Infant Death Syndrome. She was only four weeks old.

We lived on our farm then. The night Jane died my dad got up to take my brother to the bathroom and when he came back Jane wasn't breathing. He yelled something like, "Jane isn't breathing!" I woke right up and jumped out of bed and I ran right in there. Mom tried mouth-to-mouth resuscitation and it didn't work. Then a whole bunch of people came over and the doctor said she was dead.

You don't really expect to be wakened up to find that your sister is dead, and it was really confusing because I didn't want to believe she was dead and neither did anyone else. It was surprising. I felt like it's not happening. It can't be true. She's sleeping or something.

I started feeling sad right away when I saw my mom crying into Jane's little blanket. We cried for a long time. Later, Mom and Dad took my brother and I to our friends' house and the kids took us upstairs to play and that helped.

My dad and my mom made the coffin themselves and lined it with a beautiful lining Mom made. My dad dug the hole Jane was buried in and after the priest read some things they lowered her into the hole, and we threw all sorts of leaves and nuts and a lot of chestnuts in with her. My mom read a poem she had written called "No Tears for Baby Jane." My brother and I liked getting to do something for the ceremony.

I know lots of people get upset and angry with God if someone in their family dies, but I didn't feel that way. I somehow felt like it wasn't his fault. It was just something that happened. But I felt angry with Jane for dying—not right away, but after a

29

little while when I thought about it I got very angry with her. I just dug up an old book of mine that I had written poetry in a couple of years ago; I had written quite a few poems using angry feelings. After awhile the angry feelings went away and I don't feel that way anymore.

Around the time of Jane's death I kept having dreams like I was falling and a funny feeling in my stomach, and then I'd land in my bed. When Jane died I remember how my dad yelled; it scared me and I literally jumped in the air and landed on my bed. It gave me a funny feeling in my stomach.

For a while after Jane died, I was scared that Mom or Dad would die, too, or my little brother, Jack. Jack was the main one. I kept asking Mom, "Is Jack gonna be okay? Is Jack gonna be okay?" Even now I get kind of scared sometimes about my mom or my dad. I worry about them if they're a little bit late. I start getting paranoid. But it's not as scary as right after Jane died.

It was hard to go back to school after Jane died because I had brought her in and shared her with the class after she was born. It was hard to go back because they had seen her. But it was helpful to be back, too. It was easier to be there than to be home with nothing to do. And it helped that the kids just treated me normal and didn't act like, "Oh, she wants to be alone." They got me into activities. I talked to a counselor in the third grade and she helped me sort out how I was feeling after Jane died.

The hardest thing about losing Jane is seeing my whole family go through it and feeling the same things myself but not knowing how to fix it. It's very confusing. The day of her death and her birthday are hard for the whole family every year. Everyone kind of slows down and gets a little upset again. It's probably the hardest thing I've been through. It probably would be harder if we had her longer, but it was still hard.

If I want to talk about Jane I can usually talk with Mom. I remember it was real helpful after Jane died to crawl up on Mom's lap and cry with her.

One special memory I have of Jane is that I got to see her being born. It was really neat. When I saw her being born and knowing it was my sister, it was just a real exciting feeling. I remember that she liked animals with big eyes. We have a bear with huge eyes that she absolutely loved. Mom was just beginning to let me change her diapers and stuff like that. I kept one of

Jane's blankets and always use it for my stuffed animals.

Since Jane died I feel older, like I've been through a lot more. It's amazing. Everything inside you gets messed up and things don't seem like they really are for a while.

The lonely thing is that nobody I've ever met has ever lost a brother or sister. So I sometimes feel that I just wish there was someone my age that would know what I mean. It's fine to have adults you can talk to, but it's also nice to have someone your own age that can say, "I know what you mean," and can share with you the way you feel so I don't feel like I'm the only one my age who's gone through this.

One question I have since my sister died is, "When does it stop hurting?" My mom said, "someday," and that helped. After five years, it still hurts but not as much, not as intensely as it did. I think it never completely stops hurting, but it doesn't hurt as much.

Your friend,

Martha

Martha

Dear Friend,

My name is Jack. I'm nine years old. When I was four, my baby sister, Jane, died of Sudden Infant Death. She was a month old. Her heart stopped beating and her lungs stopped breathing because they were so small.

She died during the night. I didn't know what was happening. My mom tried to do mouth-to-mouth resuscitation but Jane was already dead. My mom and dad ran downstairs to the phone and called the ambulance and the state police and then they went to the hospital to see if they could find out what was causing it. I went to my next-door neighbor's farm with my other sister, Martha, and we spent the morning there. When I found out that Jane died, I felt really sad. I cried. The whole family cried.

We drove up to the funeral house in our old truck and waited for some of our friends to come. There was a guy there who was funny. He made us laugh for a long time.

My dad made the coffin. He made it out of wood—oak. At the burial we took some acorns and some leaves and stuff and dropped them over the coffin and then my mom put one of Jane's blankets over the top. Then we put some sand in the grave and in the next couple of weeks they had the gravestone on.

We have a necklace that has Jane's name on it. My sister, Martha, has a couple of Jane's blankets. I kept a little race car I bought for her when she was born. It's plastic and it squeaks.

I remember one day I was pushing her along the lawn and by accident the carriage tipped over and she fell out and she was in the grass. I started crying because I thought she was hurt and she just looked at me. She didn't even cry.

I used to call her hands windwipers because when she cried her hands would go like windwipers, like windshield wipers.

The hardest thing about losing Jane is that I can't play with her. I used to play with her every morning before I went to nursery school. And it was really hard that my mom and dad got divorced so quickly after Jane died. I felt mad at my parents after she was buried because we had to sell the farm and I had to leave my dad. Then everyone would take us different places. It was getting confusing.

You feel frustrated when your sister dies. I wish she was there because then she'd be the youngest child and it'd be nice. You want to have brothers and sisters—lots of them. I wanted to have a big family—like we would have had three children. It would have been nice. You feel frustrated that she couldn't live longer.

After awhile you get over it. You don't forget it, but once in awhile you wish that she was there and then you think of other things to do. You get over being sad after awhile, but it took a long time.

Sincerely, your friend,

Jack

"Dance, then, wherever you may be"

A letter from Brett

Dear Friend,

My name is Brett. I know what it's like to lose a little sister. When I was five years old, my sister, Wende, died of leukemia. She was three and a half. I'm thirteen now and I guess I started to really realize what had happened when I was about eight. When you're five you think only old people die and it's going to be a long time before you see your sister.

I remember when I found out she died. I was at my kindergarten picnic standing in line at the drinking fountain. My parents drove up and when they got out of the car I saw my mom was crying and they didn't have Wende with them. I knew she had died.

Even though she was real sick for a long time and I knew it had to happen sometime, I wasn't really expecting it. A couple more years is what the doctors said. I felt kind of empty. At the funeral I stood next to one of my uncles. It's the first time I'd ever seen him cry and you realize that if a grownup man had to be crying then something really sad was happening.

I kind of felt like it was the doctor's fault, that they lied to us because they said she would live to be five and then she died just after that. And I think I used to blame God. I kind of hated him a little bit. But now I realize that if he wanted her then I guess it was the best way to go because she died at home in her carriage, so at least it was peaceful.

After Wende died I really didn't talk much about her. I just kind of went on knowing deep down that she would never come back, but not really showing that. I always used to pray for her every night that she had a big wheel to ride around in. She liked big wheels. I think of Wende as being in heaven, but it's hard to

33

envision someplace you've never seen.

It was kind of hard to be with my best friend after Wende died because his brother was exactly the same age as Wende, and to see him and his brother fight was hard to take because I missed my sister so much. I'm sure we fought but I would say to myself, "If I still had my sister, I would be so nice to her." It was hard for a couple of years when I was the only child and there wasn't anyone else at home. And it was hard to do things that Wende and I used to do together, like playing out in the sprinkler.

Ever since Wende died I don't like going to hospitals or the doctor's office or for blood tests or shots in general—it's almost a hatred. It's kind of dumb to hate a blood test but that's what determined my sister was going to die.

When my mom told me that I was going to have another brother or sister after Wende died I was sort of glad but I sort of didn't want to have another one because I didn't want to lose another one. Since Wende died, I've had a little brother and then a little sister. It was hard to watch them go through the age when Wende got sick and died. But probably what's helped me the most is having another brother and sister.

Sometimes I talk with my parents about Wende and that helps. We've talked more lately than right after she died. Also, it helped to visit the cemetery. It kind of made it a lot easier. It felt like you were around her. I picked these wild daisies that were growing around and put them on her grave. There was this guy named Reggie who had a grave near Wende's. He was a kid, too, and I guess he was real good at basketball. His grave said something about that. I used to take care of her grave and his. On Wende's grave, it has Snoopy dancing. He's dancing real fast. It says, "Dance, then, wherever you may be, for I am the Lord of the dance, said he." Wende liked Snoopy.

Your friend through a shared
experience in life,

Brett

Brett

The 4th of July reminds me of Eric

A letter from Megan

Dear Friend,

My name is Megan. I'm nine years old. When I was real little, only about one and a half, my big brother, Eric, died. He was six years old. He drowned at some friend's swimming pool.

I don't remember what it was like when he died but I know what it's like now. It's like all the good times we could have had went down the drain forever.

After Eric died his body was burned and his ashes were put in a little box and buried in the ground at the cemetery. Sometimes I visit his grave at the cemetery with my mom. I read the marker with his name on it and it feels sad.

I think my brother would be a real good friend. I wish I knew what he was like, what his voice sounded like, if he was nice or mean or kind or something. I think of him the way he looked in the picture we have of him and me sitting together on my mom's bed. He's just sitting there putting his arm around me and holding his teddy bear.

Sometimes when I think of Eric I feel sad. I don't feel angry. Just sad and alone and feeling sad because most of the people I talk to haven't lost a brother or sister. They don't know what the feeling feels like. Eric wasn't my mom's brother. He was her son, but she understands how the sadness feels. I can talk with her and she listens and makes me feel like it's okay to feel sad and cry.

The Fourth of July reminds me of Eric because that's when he was born. On the Fourth of July, I feel sad and happy at the same time. Pictures of him and me and Mom all together remind me of Eric, too, and his teddy bear, Dr. DeBruin, and toy airplanes and two trucks which are in our backyard and rusted.

The hardest part of going through this is the times when you feel alone with your sadness. That's why it helps me to talk to my mom or to some friends I have who say, "I know it feels bad. I understand why you're crying." Some kids might be shy to talk about it because they can't get up the nerve to say they're sorry or anything about it. They just get really shy.

But the sadness isn't there all the time. It just comes for a little while and then I sort of get out of it, get the feeling out, and feel happy again and later on have fun. Sometimes my mom feels sad when she thinks about Eric and I give her a hug.

A little while after Eric died, my mom and dad got divorced. A few years later my mom remarried and now I have a new baby sister. It's a new experience to have a little sister. I only had a big brother.

Sincerely yours,

Megan

Megan

Jerry's heart was the one in the middle

Letters from Annette and Brian

Dear Friend,

My name is Annette. I'm thirteen years old. When I was twelve, my thirteen-year-old brother, Jerry, died by accidentally strangling himself with a rope. Here's a picture of all my brothers and sisters just a year before he died— Jerry's in the striped shirt; Mike, Cindy, and Linda are in the back row; I'm standing next to my big brother Jim, my sister, Karen, and my little brother, Brian.

When I found out Jerry died, I was shocked. I didn't think he was ever going to die. I felt terrible. I didn't want to eat or nothing. I didn't feel like doing anything. I felt like I lost my best friend.

At the funeral I kept thinking he was just going to sit up and walk away. It was the first thing I really cried at. It just seemed like the tears kept coming. I remember during the burial the priest reached down and took a rose from the family bouquet and gave it to me, and that helped.

When Jerry died I was mad at God. Like, "Why did you pick Jerry to die? Why couldn't you pick somebody else?" But Mom said, "Well, if he would have picked somebody else like Brian or you, we would have missed you just as much."

And I was mad at myself, really. I thought I should have been there because he was supposed to be cleaning the barn, and I kept kicking myself that I wasn't out there to help him because I thought if I was there it wouldn't have happened.

After Jerry died I kept feeling afraid to die. I didn't want to die but yet I did because I wanted to see Jerry. When I'd go to bed I just couldn't sleep because I'd feel like God was going to take me then. I was afraid I was going to die or somebody would come and kill me or something like that. It lasted quite awhile and then finally went away, but while it was happening I couldn't sleep and kept crying and everything else. Now I'm not as afraid anymore because I realize that you have to die sometime, and I don't have nightmares anymore.

I miss Jerry. I feel kind of lonely but yet I don't, because I feel like he's there watching me. But it's just not the same. Jerry was the joker. He would always tease me and act really funny. When I was three years old he taught me how to tie my shoes because he didn't like tying shoes. Every time he had his shoe untied he always called me and then I'd tie his shoe.

After Jerry died, my friends helped by being kinder to me. It was hard if they kept bringing up what happened, but they kind of left it if I didn't want to talk about it. They helped me out at school when I was so tense from losing Jerry that I started feeling like I didn't want to go to school. My friends helped me through that and helped me with homework if I needed help. I had trouble going to school for about a month after Jerry died. The teacher helped me get through it, too. She was close to Jerry and she just knew what it felt like.

When Jerry died I felt like the whole world was against me and that nobody liked me or anything because, you know, I lost my best friend. But then I started to realize that not everybody's against you, they're more for you. When my friends were kinder to me, that made me feel good, that not everybody was against me. And my family helped because I knew they were going through the same thing—that it wasn't just me. Sometimes I'd get the sadness or madness out by crying or playing games or eating.

Since Jerry died I'm not so tense when somebody dies. I still cry and stuff but I'm able to cope better. Like last week my aunt died and I realized since I lost Jerry that they'll be up there together watching over everything. That helped me get through it all.

When your brother dies it feels like the whole world is caving in on you. You think about it and you cry a lot but that doesn't help much. I think it hurts for the rest of your life, but you start to cope with it better in about a month. But it will always be with you

I feel happier because I know Jerry's up there with God. Now I can even think about him sometimes without crying.

Love,

Annette

Annette

Dear Friend,

My name is Brian. I am eight years old. When I was six years old my big brother, Jerry, accidentally hanged himself and died. He was thirteen years old. It happened out in the barn. I was in the house. My brother, Mike, called and I came out with my mother and my sister and saw what happened. The ambulance came and took him to the hospital to see if they could get him back but they couldn't. When Mom and Dad came back and told us he died I felt pretty sad.

I remember my mom put a cross, his rosary, and a heart in his coffin. The heart was cross-stitched with his name on it and lace around it. My mom made one for each of us and hung them on the bulletin boards in our bedrooms. Jerry shared a room with Mike and me. Our hearts were glued together at the lace. Mom tore Jerry's off to put it in the coffin. His heart was the one in the middle. Then there was an empty space between me and Mike's hearts.

When Jerry died I felt very sad. It's not very fun to lose a brother. And I felt afraid. It's like when you're the only one in your bedroom and you're only about four and you're scared that a monster's going to come out and get you. Something like that. At first I felt more scared than now. It was like a switch at night. It'd come and go, come and go. Now it just depends. When I found out my sister was going to move away I felt real sad. When I heard that I said, "Oh, no." I felt real scared.

I miss Jerry because we did a lot of stuff together. We got in trouble for bouncing on the bed. We'd roll around and jump up and come back down. It was fun. Jerry taught me how to fish. First he taught me how to put a worm on, which I hate. Then he taught me how to throw it, how to cast it. We had a pretty nice time. One time I caught Jerry by mistake. I was throwing out the line and I caught him. He showed me how to build things, too. We'd build little animal pens together. And sometimes we'd fight.

I remember Jerry's favorite toys were his dinosaur and shark. He got a lot of trophies from baseball and football. And he liked pigs a lot. He showed them at the county fair. When I see pigs I think of Jerry.

I still dream about Jerry a little bit. Sometimes they're not so good and sometimes they're okay. It just depends what kind of night you're on. If it's a happy dream, I feel a lot better. Sometimes I feel sad about Jerry all of a sudden. At first I'm real happy and then I feel sad. When that happens I just kind of hang around. If I'm home I go up to my bedroom and lay down and cry for a little bit and that helps.

When Jerry died it felt like nothing was going right and now it's pretty much going right again. It still hurts some but not as much.

Love,

Brian

Brian